Dates of a Decade

THE 1980s

Joseph Harris

FRANKLIN WATTS
LONDON • SYDNEY

First printed in paperback in 2013

First published in 2009 by Franklin Watts

Copyright © 2009 Arcturus Publishing Limited

Franklin Watts
338 Euston Road
London NW1 3BH

Franklin Watts Australia
Level 17/207 Kent Street, Sydney, NSW 2000

Produced by Arcturus Publishing Limited,
26/27 Bickels Yard, 151–153 Bermondsey Street,
London SE1 3HA

Series concept: Alex Woolf
Editor and picture researcher: Alex Woolf
Designer: Phipps Design

Picture credits:
Corbis: cover *centre* (Neal Preston), cover *left* and 10, 13 (Roger Ressmeyer), 14
(Bettmann), 17 (David Rubinger), 18 (Bettmann), 19 (Jean Louis Atlan/Sygma), 22
(Peter Turnley), 23 (Peter Turnley), 24 (Reuters), 25 (Bettmann), 26, 27 (Bettmann),
28 (Igor Kostin/Sygma), 29 (Igor Kostin/Sygma), 30 (Reuters), 31 (CinemaPhoto), 32
(Reuters), 33 (Reuters), 36 (Peter Turnley), 37 (Bettmann), cover *right* and 38
(Reuters), 39 (David Turnley), 44 (Bryn Colton/Assignments Photographers), 45
(Bryn Colton/Assignments Photographers).
Getty Images: 4, 5 (Popperfoto), 6 (AFP), 7 (AFP), 9, 11 (Time & Life Pictures), 12
(AFP), 15, 16 (AFP), 21 (AFP), 41 (AFP), 42 (Popperfoto), 43.
Shutterstock: 34 (Daniele DM), 35 (TAOLMOR).

Every attempt has been made to clear copyright. Should there be any inadvertent
omission, please apply to the publisher for rectification.

A CIP catalogue record for this book is available from the British Library.

Dewey Decimal Classification Number: 909.82' 8

ISBN 978 1 4451 1882 6

Printed in China

Franklin Watts is a division of Hachette Children's Books,
an Hachette Livre UK company.
www.hachettelivre.co.uk

Supplier 03, Date 0213, Print Run 2351
SL000838EN

Contents

GLOBAL EVENTS

BRITISH EVENTS

Mugabe Wins Zimbabwean Elections

The elections were the first to be held in Zimbabwe Rhodesia in which the black majority had an opportunity to take real power. The victory of Robert Mugabe and his ZANU (Zimbabwe African National Union) party marked the end of years of domination by the country's white minority. Not long before, Mugabe had been a guerrilla leader in the bush, hunted by government forces. Now he would become prime minister. Many people regarded him as a dangerous extremist, but the election result showed that the black majority overwhelmingly supported ZANU and rejected the past.

Illegal independence

Zimbabwe Rhodesia had been a British colony until 1965. It was known first as Southern Rhodesia and later simply as Rhodesia, after the British empire-builder Cecil Rhodes. The largely self-governing colony was ruled by the privileged white minority. In the 1960s they began to fear that the British government would give the vote to the black majority and then grant the colony independence. To stop this from happening, in 1965 the Rhodesian government, led by Ian Smith, issued a Unilateral (one-sided) Declaration of Independence (UDI) from Britain.

6th March 1980: Dr Robert Gabriel Mugabe, newly elected President of Zimbabwe, holds a press conference in his garden in Mount Pleasant, Salisbury.

The intention was clearly to keep Rhodesia under white control. Britain declared the UDI illegal, and most countries condemned Smith's racist regime. Sanctions (limits on trade) were imposed to hurt Rhodesia's economy, but Rhodesia was helped by similar, neighbouring racist regimes, notably South Africa.

The regime weakens

Black Rhodesians responded by forming two guerrilla movements, Mugabe's ZANU and Joshua Nkomo's ZAPU. By the late 1970s, Smith's government was weakened by international pressure and long 'bush wars' against the guerrillas, and it finally began to make concessions. Rhodesia was renamed Zimbabwe Rhodesia (after an ancient city built before whites settled the country) in 1979 and a black-majority government was elected, led by Bishop Abel Muzorewa. However, Smith had arranged matters so that real power remained in the hands of the whites. Finally, however, in early 1980, he was forced to allow elections in which power would pass to the winner and the guerrilla groups would take part. ZANU took 57 and ZAPU 20 of the 80 seats elected by the black population. The name 'Rhodesia' was dropped and the country became Zimbabwe.

As prime minister, Mugabe promised to treat the white minority fairly. However, he failed to live up to his promises, and Zimbabwe was to suffer greatly from his increasingly despotic rule.

Jubilant supporters of Robert Mugabe celebrate his election victory and the transfer of real political power from a white elite to the black majority.

What the papers said

The great gamble in Zimbabwe Rhodesia is over. The result is presumably not what those who staked so much [Smith and his followers] can have hoped. They may nonetheless still hope that the consequences will not be as dire as might be expected. Mr Mugabe is in fact an unknown quantity. How he will turn out is unpredictable, as it always seems to be with Africans who get power.... If Mr Mugabe disappoints his ... friends and delights his opponents, he will not be the first African to do so. We must hope he will do both.

Daily Telegraph, 5 March 1980

• **FURTHER INFORMATION**
📖 Books:
Global Hotspots Zimbabwe
by Yvonne Thorper (Macmillan Education, 2011)
🔗 Websites:
www.bbc.co.uk/news/world-africa-14113249
A good overview of the history, geography and economy of the country

Solidarity is Legalized in Poland

On 30 August 1980, Poland's communist government gave in to pressure from striking workers, who were demanding greater freedom. The deputy prime minister, Mieczyslaw Jagielski, met with the leader of the strike, Lech Walesa, and other workers' representatives at the northern city of Gdansk. They made the 'Gdansk Agreement', which permitted workers to form their own trade union, independent of the state and free to take strike action. This was an extraordinary event, since communist states normally refused to tolerate any kind of opposition and allowed only government-controlled unions to operate.

The government's failure

In Poland, communism had been established in 1945, at the end of World War II, by the Soviet Union. Poland became part of the East European communist bloc. The Polish communists were in fact a small minority, and communism never became genuinely popular. However, it was economic failure that seriously undermined the government's authority in 1980. Living standards were already low, and in July, when the government increased the cost of basic commodities, discontent became serious.

At the Lenin shipyard in Gdansk, a popular crane operator, Anna Walentynowicz, was fired. For the disgruntled workforce, this was the final straw. An unemployed electrician named Lech Walesa emerged as the leader of the protesting workers, who occupied the shipyard. They held it for two months, resisting government attempts to divide them by making limited concessions. The news spread, and in August strikes sprang up right across Poland.

The leader of the Solidarity movement, Lech Walesa, addresses an assembly of his supporters outside the gates of the Lenin shipyard in Gdansk.

Solidarity

If the strikers had tried to fight the government, the army – or the Soviet Union – would have crushed them. Instead, they negotiated and sometimes co-operated with the authorities. For a time, the strategy worked. Following the Gdansk Agreement, the independent trade union Solidarity was formally established in September, with Walesa as its president. Millions of Poles joined it. However, the economic situation remained bleak and the Soviet Union pressed the Polish government to end the 'Solidarity experiment', fearing that people in other communist countries might try to follow its example.

In December 1981 the Polish military, led by General Wojciech Jaruzelski, acted. They carried out mass arrests of Solidarity activists, proclaimed martial law, and drove Solidarity underground. Despite this, the movement had played an important role in showing the fragility of communist dictatorships. It re-emerged in the late 1980s as East European communism collapsed. In 1990, Lech Walesa became the president of a free Poland.

Polish Prime Minister Wojciech Jaruzelski announces martial law during a televised address from Warsaw on 13 December 1981. The decree set up a new ruling body, the Military Council of National Salvation.

⊙ eye witness

The actual signing of the … agreement was scheduled for the great assembly hall on Monday, August 31. With a minimum of ceremony both sides signed the papers…. On the Monday morning, the first trade union office was opened…. The rooms were on the first floor of a decrepit office block with creaking floorboards…. It was some months before the rest of the country was prepared to recognize the idea of free trade unions…. The capital of a new workers' Poland had moved to the Baltic coast.

Lech Walesa, *A Path of Hope* (Collins Harvill, 1987)

- **SEE ALSO**
  Pages 38–39: 10 November 1989
  The Berlin Wall Comes Down

- **FURTHER INFORMATION**
  📖 Books:
  Poland by J Kadziolka
  (Cherrytree Books, 2005)
  🖰 Websites:
  www.solidarity.gov.pl
  A multimedia site illustrating the history of Solidarity

Iran and Iraq Go to War

There had been skirmishes for some time between Iraqi and Iranian forces in their disputed border territories. Then, on 22 September, Iraq suddenly launched air strikes on Iranian airfields and began a full-scale land invasion. Iran's air force struck back, and Iranian troops and militiamen were rushed to the front. Iraq's dictator, Saddam Hussein, hoped for a rapid victory, but the war turned into a long, bloody and futile conflict.

The enemies

Iraq and Iran were both Muslim nations, but in important respects they were very different. Iraq was a secular state in which religion had relatively little influence on political policies. By contrast, Iran's supreme authority was a senior Muslim figure, the Ayatollah Khomeini, who had headed the country's 'Islamic Revolution' in 1979. As a result, Iranian society was run on strict religious lines, and many aspects of the Western, and especially American, way of life were condemned and outlawed.

Since Khomeini wished to spread the Islamic Revolution to other lands, the United States and many other Western countries supported Iraq in the conflict. However, the Western nations had underestimated Saddam's ambition to control the Persian Gulf, which was the key to the region's vast oil wealth. The immediate cause of the conflict between Iraq and Iran was a shared waterway leading into the Gulf, the Shatt al-Arab, claimed by Iraq. Saddam also hoped to seize the oil-rich Iranian province of Khuzestan.

eye witness

We managed to catch glimpses of the Iranian Air Force in action here in Baghdad…. I was woken by a persistent sound … like someone wearing hobnail boots clattering down a concrete staircase. It was, in fact, anti-aircraft fire echoing around the city and coming from batteries placed on buildings a hundred yards away. From my hotel balcony I saw two American-built Phantom jets flying at a tremendous speed straight at me…. At night the city is blacked out – we have to write our reports, this one included, by candlelight.

Michael Vestey in Tony Grant (editor), *From Our Own Correspondent* (Pan, 1995)

Stalemate

The Iraqi advance was soon halted and their forces were then driven back. By 1982, Saddam was ready to make peace and it was Iran that insisted on continuing the conflict. The war turned into a stalemate. Defensive lines, bristling with machine guns, prevented both sides from securing a permanent advantage. Both used any means

Iraqi dictator Saddam Hussein addresses his forces before the invasion of Iran. The attack led to an eight-year war.

available. Iraq employed chemical weapons, while the Iranians sent barely trained conscripts to advance in human waves against the enemy lines. Cities were subjected to aerial bombardment, causing many civilian casualties. Nothing could break the deadlock, and in 1988 the UN finally brokered a ceasefire.

In 1990, when Saddam invaded Kuwait and became the West's deadly enemy, he made peace with Iran. After the loss of a million or more lives, the frontiers remained the same as they had been in 1980. Saddam was eventually toppled in 2003.

- **FURTHER INFORMATION**
- 📖 Books:
  The First Gulf War, 1990–1991
  by Steve Crawford (Brown Bear Reference, 2008)
- 🖰 Websites:
  http://news.bbc.co.uk/1/hi/world/middle_east/
  4260420.stm
  The Iran-Iraq war 25 years on

Reagan is Elected US President

On 4 November, 1980, the Republican Party's candidate, Ronald Reagan, swept to victory in the US presidential election. He trounced the sitting president, Democrat Jimmy Carter, so thoroughly that Carter conceded defeat even before polling had finished in some places. Carter had come to be seen as a weak leader, especially since he had failed to rescue American hostages held in Iran. Reagan was 69, a former Hollywood actor and governor of California. Though relaxed and soft-spoken, he seemed a tough character who offered America strong leadership.

The Cold War

Reagan was sworn in as president on 20 January 1981. He had a notable early success, agreeing a deal with Iran that secured the release of the hostages. He also made important changes in US foreign policy. Since 1945, two superpowers, the United States and the communist Soviet Union, had competed for global supremacy. Each possessed an arsenal of fearsomely destructive weapons. Despite a long 'Cold War' of hostility and suspicion, the USA and the Soviet Union had not come to blows, and in the 1970s there had even been some easing of tensions between them.

Ronald Reagan and his wife Nancy wave to supporters on 20 January 1981, celebrating the new president's inauguration.

Reagan, however, was militantly anti-communist. He labelled the Soviet Union the 'evil empire' and supported anti-communist groups all round the world. He even adopted a controversial plan – nicknamed 'Star Wars' – to construct a defensive system in space. Though critics of Reagan's policies felt that they risked a world war, they came at a time when the Soviet Union was in economic decline and in no position to respond aggressively. In fact, during his second term as president, Reagan negotiated significant arms reductions with the Soviet Union. By the time he left office in 1989, the Cold War was coming to an end.

'Reaganomics'

Reagan also changed the direction of government policy at home. His ideas, often described as 'Reaganomics', reflected the views of many conservatives. Reagan believed that the government interfered too much in people's lives. He wanted less regulation of business activity and favoured tax cuts to encourage people to buy more and stimulate economic growth. Supporters of these policies held that, in the long run, they would benefit everybody, whereas critics argued that while they made the rich richer, the poor were left behind. Reagan's policies were similar to those of Margaret Thatcher in Britain and helped set the tone for the 'consumerist' 1980s.

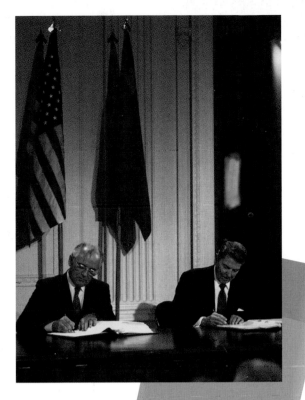

President Ronald Reagan (right) and Soviet leader Mikhail Gorbachev sign an arms reduction agreement in the East Room of the White House.

⊙ eye witness

It is painful even now to recall those last two days of the campaign, and the dismal results that I had to face on election night. After ... it became clear that the hostages [in Iran] would not be freed, Rosalynn [Carter's wife] and I knew my support had sharply fallen ... we did not anticipate the magnitude of our defeat. To lose all but six states and to have our party rejected ... were additional embarrassments for me.... At least it was a relief that the political campaign was over.

Jimmy Carter, *Keeping Faith* (Collins, 1982)

- **SEE ALSO**
  Pages 22–23: 11 March 1985
  Gorbachev Becomes Soviet Leader
  Pages 30–31: 19 October 1987
  World Stock Exchanges Crash

- **FURTHER INFORMATION**
  📖 Books:
  Ronald Reagan: Our Fortieth President
  by Cynthia Amoroso
  (Child's World, 2008)
  Websites:
  www.whitehouse.gov/about/presidents
  A site with a biography and links to the Ronald Reagan archives

The IBM PC is Released

On 12 August 1981, the world's leading computer manufacturer, IBM, announced that it had developed a new product, the personal computer, or PC. It was said to be an affordable computer system that would appeal to home users and small businesses. Rival companies, such as Commodore, Atari and Apple, had already released machines aimed at these markets, but the IBM machine was the direct ancestor of the PCs used today. The development of the IBM PC started a technological revolution that led to the introduction of computers into homes and businesses worldwide.

The 1981 IBM PC appears primitive compared to today's computers, but was cutting-edge technology at the time.

A variety of computers were developed in the 1980s, thanks to IBM's decision not to use all their own components. Instead, hurrying to develop their PC, they built it with parts bought from other manufacturers such as Intel, and software provided by Microsoft. Other corporations were free to buy such products and use them in their own PCs. Consequently, the PC market became highly competitive, forcing the pace of change.

The computer age

By the early 1980s, computers were able to handle huge amounts of information at a speed that humans could not match. Their impact on every aspect of human activity was bound to be immense. Very powerful computers had been developed before the 1980s, but the machines were very large and expensive, and operating them required special skills. Only governments and big corporations used them. The development of the PC in the 1980s was to make computers part of everyday life.

The PC revolution

Despite its lower price, the first IBM PC was still too expensive for most home users, but it sold in unexpectedly large numbers to businesses. This marked the beginning of a workplace revolution that accelerated as computers became increasingly user-friendly. The PC's word-processing programs made it possible to correct and reorganize text and information, and PCs swiftly replaced typewriters. Similarly, computer databases replaced paper-based systems of data storage.

PCs very quickly became standard office equipment. This photo, from 1986, shows workers at a US Internal Revenue Service office entering data from tax forms into computers.

PCs continued to become cheaper and more powerful, and by the later 1980s PCs were invading the home, offering not only word processing but also increasingly complex and ingenious games. The microprocessors that lay at the heart of the IBM PC also allowed the development of other technologies. Many of these, such as mobile telephones and portable CD players, became familiar features of everyday life.

What the papers said

International Business Machines of the US, the leader in the world market for large computers, yesterday made its long-awaited entry into the booming market for personal computers. The company unveiled a small machine, called the IBM Personal Computer, which will sell for only $1,565 (£860) in its most basic version and up to about $6,000 with all the trimmings. The computer industry has been speculating for months about the IBM machine, which will provide formidable competition for many products already on the market.

Ian Hargreaves, *Financial Times*, 13 August 1981

- **SEE ALSO**
  Pages 24–25: 13 July 1985
  The Live Aid Concerts

  Pages 30-31: 19 October 1987
  World Stock Exchanges Crash

- **FURTHER INFORMATION**
- 📖 Books:
  The History of the Computer by Elizabeth Raum (Heinemann, 2008)
- 🖱 Websites:
  inventors.about.com/library/blcoindex.htm
  Covers the major developments in computer technology

Argentina Invades the Falklands

Early in the morning of 2 April 1982, the Argentines landed at three places on the main island, East Falkland. The 940 Argentines, equipped with troop carriers and transport vehicles, faced 81 British defenders, most of them Royal Marines. The first attack occurred at 5.30 a.m. By 9.30 the British, surrounded in Government House, had surrendered. The only casualties were one dead and two wounded Argentines.

Disputed sovereignty

The Falklands island group lies in the South Atlantic, 450 kilometres off the coast of Argentina. Their British-descended inhabitants wanted the Falklands to remain a British colony. The Argentines argued that, geographically, the islands were part of their country, stolen by the British.

After years of talks, Argentina's ruling junta (military council) acted. In power since 1976, the junta had murdered thousands of opponents and was deeply unpopular. It invaded the Falklands in the hope of winning support for the régime, and the Argentine people did in fact greet the news with wild patriotic enthusiasm. The junta calculated that the British government would protest, but would not fight for a group of far-away, insignificant islands.

The war

The junta was wrong. The British government, led by Margaret Thatcher, sent a fleet carrying 30,000 troops. It sailed the 13,000 kilometres to the Falklands and recaptured the islands in June 1982, along with the even more remote island of South Georgia, which the Argentines had also occupied.

The heaviest casualties occurred during engagements at sea. The Argentines made effective use of Exocet missiles, sinking the British destroyer HMS *Sheffield*. However, the Argentine navy was not strong enough to face the British fleet in battle. Britain defined an 'exclusion zone' – any Argentine vessel appearing in this area would be deemed a

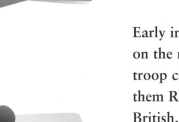

A rally is held in the Plaza de Mayo in the Argentine capital, Buenos Aires, to boost morale following the British recapture of South Georgia on 19 April.

legitimate target. In the war's most controversial incident, a British submarine sank the Argentine cruiser *General Belgrano*, with 323 hands lost, although the vessel was outside the exclusion zone and heading away from it. However, the *General Belgrano* was under orders to attack the British navy and, in 1994, the Argentine government conceded that the sinking was a legal act of war. On land, British troops overcame the Argentine forces after some sharp encounters, notably at Goose Green.

The aftermath

Compared with most wars, the death toll (fewer than 1,000) was small. The political consequences were important, however. Victory boosted the fortunes of Margaret Thatcher's previously unpopular government and helped her to win the 1983 election. By contrast, the humiliation of defeat destroyed the junta. Its head, General Leopoldo Galtieri, resigned, and the junta itself collapsed soon afterwards. By 1983, Argentina had returned to democracy.

A line of British soldiers advances during the campaign to win back the Falklands. 258 British troops lost their lives in the conflict.

⊙ eye witness

It all went just as though we were on an exercise…. My group of four Amtracs [armoured troop carriers] approached the beach in a diamond formation. If I got ashore safely, the others would form a column and follow me in…. All went well. The beach was incredibly white, to my surprise, with a steep slope ten metres from the waterline, a few rocks; there was no cover for my huge Amtrac, and I thought I was a sitting duck as I came up that slope – but the place was deserted.

Lieutenant-Commander Hugo Santillón, in Martin Middlebrook, *The Argentine Fight for the Falklands* (Pen & Sword Books, 2003)

- **FURTHER INFORMATION**
- 📖 Books:
  Argentina by Charles J Shields
  (Mason Crest Publishers, 2009)
- 🖱 Websites:
  www.falklandswar.org.uk
  A site about the war from a British point of view

Massacres in Lebanon

Between 16 and 18 September, militias linked with a Lebanese political party, the Phalange, carried out massacres that horrified the world. The victims were Palestinian refugees who lived in two camps, Sabra and Shatila, on the edge of the Lebanese capital, Beirut. The condition of the corpses showed that the killings had been carried out in a particularly savage fashion. Entire families, including children, had been wiped out. The number of deaths was never reliably established, and estimates ranged between 700 and 3,500.

Turmoil in Lebanon

At this time, Lebanon was in a chaotic state. Lebanese political life was based on Christians and Muslims sharing power, but this arrangement was showing signs of breaking down. The situation was complicated by the existence of camps like Sabra and Shatila, housing Palestinian refugees from neighbouring Israel. The camps also served as bases for the PLO (Palestine Liberation Organization), which conducted cross-border terrorist and guerrilla operations against Israel. The PLO also played a part in the power struggles within Lebanon, in conflict with Christian militias such as the Phalangists.

A Palestinian woman weeps as the body of one of her relatives is carried away on a stretcher following the Phalangist assault on the Sabra refugee camp.

Invasion and massacres

In June 1982, Israeli forces invaded Lebanon to drive out the PLO. The Christian militias were their allies. The Israelis besieged the PLO's strongholds in West Beirut until the PLO agreed to leave the country. By September the PLO's forces had been shipped out under international supervision. However, the Israelis suspected that there were still PLO elements in Sabra and Shatila, and the Phalangist militia was sent in to flush them out. Instead, the militiamen began a wholesale massacre, probably acting in revenge for the assassination three weeks before of a newly installed Phalangist president of Lebanon, Bashir Gemayel.

The fallout

The massacre raised serious questions about the role of the Israeli army. Were the militiamen sent in just to weed out terrorists, or did the Israelis know what was going to happen? Why didn't the army step in once the killing had started? Some 300,000 Israelis demonstrated in the streets, demanding answers. An official investigation blamed the defence minister, Ariel Sharon, for failing to foresee how the Phalangists were likely to behave. Sharon resigned, although he later made a remarkable comeback as prime minister in 2001. The Phalangist leaders were never brought to justice. Lebanon remained a flashpoint of Middle Eastern violence.

Israelis demonstrate outside the home of their prime minister, Menachem Begin, after the massacre in Beirut.

What the papers said

There are many versions of the massacre.... Some of the victims were lying among ... half-packed suitcases as if they had been trying to escape when the killers burst in. Others had obviously been taken by surprise, because there were half-eaten meals near the bodies.... Reporters said it was impossible to get an accurate estimate of the numbers of Palestinians killed because the bodies were strewn across several acres of wreckage.... Bulldozers had been used to pile wreckage on many of the bodies in an attempt to conceal them, but arms and legs were sticking out of the rubble.

Colin Smith and Eric Silver, *Observer*, 19 September 1982

• **SEE ALSO**
Pages 36–37: 4 June 1989
Massacre in Tiananmen Square

• **FURTHER INFORMATION**
📖 Books:
Lebanon by Ann Malaspina
(Chelsea House Publishers, 2009)
🖱 Websites:
www.globaleye.org.uk/secondary_spring06/
eyeon/palestinians.html
The plight of Palestinian refugees in Lebanon, with lots of useful links

The HIV Virus is Identified

On 23 April 1984 US Health Secretary Margaret Heckler announced that scientists had identified the cause of the fearful disease Aids (Acquired Immune Deficiency Syndrome). It was a virus, given the name HIV (Human Immunodeficiency Virus). HIV infected white blood cells in the bloodstream and prevented them from fighting infections. It also implanted the cells with its own genetic material, enabling the virus to multiply. The final stage of the infection, Aids, did not kill sufferers directly. They died because of the damage done to their bodies' natural defences (the immune system), which meant that even minor infections could prove fatal.

The identification of HIV was not an exclusively American feat – a French team had achieved similar results in 1983. Credit for the discovery is now shared between scientists of the two nations. It was hailed as a major breakthrough, and encouraged hopes that a cure might rapidly be found.

The first cases

Aids first came to public attention in 1981 as a nameless disorder. Previously healthy homosexual men in three American cities, Los Angeles, San Francisco and New York, showed symptoms such as extreme weight loss, leading eventually to death, often from a lung infection or rare skin cancer. Over 150 cases were identified during 1981. At first people believed the disease affected only homosexuals. Subsequently, the disease was discovered in some heterosexuals.

The disease was passed on through contact with infected blood and could be contracted through sexual intercourse or, in the case of drug users, by sharing the needles they used to

At a joint press conference, Dr Robert Gallo, a researcher at the National Cancer Institute, and Margaret Heckler, the US Health Secretary, announce that the HIV virus has been identified. Gallo led the American team that made the discovery.

The enormous Aids Memorial Quilt was created to commemorate Aids victims. Begun in 1987 in San Francisco, it is shown here during a public display in Washington, DC.

inject themselves. An infected mother could pass it to her child during pregnancy or breastfeeding. Before the dangers became apparent, some individuals contracted the disease from transfusions of infected blood.

Global epidemic

By 1985, when the World Health Organization defined Aids as an epidemic, the disease was causing widespread anxiety. Governments ran education programmes to combat misinformation and promote the use of condoms for 'safe sex'. The first treatments – not cures – appeared, but the high cost of the drugs involved were beyond the means of many poorer sufferers. Although millions were suffering globally, Africa was the hardest hit, probably because Aids had been present there for the longest time. From the 1990s, the Aids issue was being raised everywhere from the United Nations to pop concerts. Hopes of an early cure faded, and the world faced a long and painful battle against the disease.

What the papers said

The multi-million dollar hunt for the cause of Aids may soon be over but the epidemic is likely to continue spreading at an ever-increasing rate for two years or more. Barring a breakthrough in treatment, the recent discoveries by US and French scientists will have come too late to save the 2,000 surviving Aids victims and the 3,000 or more people in Europe and the US who on current trends will develop the disease this year.... The number of US cases topped 4,000 this month.

Andrew Veitch, Guardian, 25 April 1984

- **FURTHER INFORMATION**
- 📖 Books:
  Stories About Surviving HIV/AIDS by Theresa Saliba (Franklin Watts, 2010)
- Websites:
  library.thinkquest.org/J003087F/
  An all-you-need-to-know site for young people

India's Prime Minister is Assassinated

The Indian prime minister, Mrs Indira Gandhi, was murdered on 31 October 1984 by her own bodyguards. They shot her as she left her New Delhi home to meet a TV crew. The assassins were Sikhs, members of a minority religion in India, where the majority are Hindus. The killing sparked widespread violence against Sikhs, and it was in a climate of disorder that Mrs Gandhi's son Rajiv was sworn in as her successor. Mrs Gandhi was cremated three days later.

Operation Blue Star

Since achieving independence from Britain in 1947, India had enjoyed stability as the world's largest democracy. But it was a land of many peoples and religions, which sometimes created serious problems. Mrs Gandhi's assassination was an act of revenge, prompted by a military operation she had authorized four months earlier. The operation was directed against Sikh militants who aimed to win independence for their home region, the Punjab, and used terrorism to achieve their goal.

In June 1984, Indian troops surrounded the terrorist leader Jarnail Singh Bhindranwale and his followers, who had taken refuge in the Golden Temple in Amritsar. The temple was the Sikhs' holiest shrine, but after a three-day siege the Indian forces launched a direct attack. The assault, Operation Blue Star, met with ferocious resistance. Over 700 of the militants were killed in the fighting, and the temple was damaged. Many Sikhs were outraged. Among them were the previously loyal guards who killed Mrs Gandhi.

What the papers said

Mrs Gandhi was killed in the gardens of her own home as she walked towards ... her staff offices.... As she came towards her assassins, two of them greeted her with a ... bow with hands pressed together; she returned the traditional greeting. Sub-Inspector Beant Singh of the Delhi Armed Police, fired at her with his revolver.... Constable Satwant Singh emptied 30 rounds of his Sten gun at her as she lay on the ground. Both he and Inspector Beant were themselves shot by other guards.

Michael Hamlyn, *The Times*, 1 November 1984

*India's new premier,
Rajiv Gandhi (at the front of the
group with his wife and daughter), stands
before the cremation pyre of his mother, Indira
Gandhi, in New Delhi.*

A new era

When Rajiv Gandhi took office, he appealed for an end to the violence
against Sikhs. He went on to grant the Sikhs a degree of autonomy (self-
rule, but not independence) and offered to repair the Golden Temple. This
calmed the situation, although neither Sikh nor Hindu extremists were
satisfied. As prime minister, Rajiv Gandhi broke with the policies of Mrs
Gandhi and her father, Jawaharlal Nehru, who between them had ruled
India for almost the entire period since 1947. Under their
leadership many aspects of the Indian economy had been
state controlled, and India had been neutral in
international affairs and friendly with the Soviet
Union. Rajiv promoted a more competitive, less
regulated economy and moved closer to the United
States. The death of Indira Gandhi marked the end of
an era. However, the Nehru 'dynasty' continued to
dominate Indian politics in the person of Rajiv
Gandhi, until he too was assassinated in 1991.

- **FURTHER INFORMATION**
- 📖 **Books:**
  Indira Gandhi: Political Leader in India
  by Barbara A Somervill
  (Signature Lives, 2007)
- 🔗 **Websites:**
  www.sikh-history.com/sikhhist/events/
  attack841.html
  Operation Blue Star

Gorbachev Becomes Soviet Leader

On 11 March 1985, Mikhail Gorbachev became general secretary of the Central Committee of the Soviet Communist Party, a post that made him the leader of the Soviet Union. At 54, Gorbachev was comparatively young. The Soviet leaders before him, Yuri Andropov and Konstantin Chernenko, had been elderly men who had ruled for only a short time before dying. Gorbachev was chosen because of a general recognition that dynamic leadership was needed to re-energize a stagnant Soviet Union.

Soviet premier Mikhail Gorbachev greets an enthusiastic crowd in Prague in the former Czechoslovakia.

Soviet problems

The Soviet Union was dominated by the Communist Party, which suppressed all opposition and made any political changes difficult to achieve. Some past crimes and mistakes, especially under the dictatorship of Joseph Stalin (1928–1953), had been admitted. But much was still covered up, and the Soviet Union remained a secretive society. Moreover, by the 1970s the country was suffering from severe economic problems. The Soviet Union's centralized, state-run economy was highly inefficient, and struggled to cope with the pressures of its military rivalry with the United States. The Soviet Union led an alliance of communist states in competition with the United States and its allies. In this 'Cold War', both sides spent vast sums on nuclear and other armaments, as well as propping up weaker allies and seeking to influence uncommitted nations. By the mid-1980s, around 15–17 per cent of the Soviet Union's gross national product (total value of all its goods and services) was spent on defence.

Gorbachev's reforms

To tackle the problems, Gorbachev proclaimed new policies of perestroika (restructuring the Soviet economy) and glasnost (openness). The economy was decentralized, giving local authorities and businesspeople more responsibility. Facts about the country's past and present were revealed. People were encouraged to express themselves freely and were promised greater choice in electing their leaders. Gorbachev sought agreement with the United States on ending the nuclear arms race and he reduced the size of the Soviet armed forces. Soviet aid to friends and allies was also cut, and Gorbachev made it clear that Soviet troops would no longer be used to rescue unpopular communist regimes.

Communist collapse

Gorbachev wished to reform, not destroy, the communist system. But economic decentralization at home was mismanaged and weakened the country further. In 1989, the communist regimes of Eastern Europe collapsed, no longer supported by the Soviet Union. The Soviet Union itself survived until 1991, when it – and Gorbachev's own career – came to an end.

Gorbachev's poorly planned reforms led to an economic crisis. Queues outside shops were a common sight as essential goods became increasingly scarce.

⊙ eye witness

On 10 March 1985, I had barely returned home after work when the telephone rang and ... informed me of Chernenko's death. After the call I ... convened [called] a Politburo meeting for 11 p.m. that night.... It was about four o'clock in the morning when I returned home. Raisa Maksimova [his wife] was waiting up for me ... my last words that night stand out in my mind: 'You see ... if I really want to change something I would have to accept the nomination [as general secretary].... We can't go on living like this.'

Mikhail Gorbachev, *Memoirs* (Doubleday, 1996)

- **SEE ALSO**
  Pages 32-33: 15 February 1989
  Soviet Troops Leave Afghanistan
  Pages 38-39: 10 November 1989
  The Berlin Wall Comes Down

- **FURTHER INFORMATION**
  📖 Books:
  Years of Russia, the USSR and the Collapse of Soviet Communism
  by Jane Jenkins (Hodder Education, 2008)
  Websites:
  www.achievement.org/autodoc/page/gor0int-1
  An interview with Gorbachev

The Live Aid Concerts

Two groundbreaking televised concerts were held on 13 July 1985 to raise money for famine victims in Africa. The event was called 'Live Aid' and was the brainchild of Bob Geldof, lead singer of the band the Boomtown Rats. Live Aid was the biggest pop event of all time. The performances at London's Wembley Stadium and Philadelphia's John F Kennedy Stadium were broadcast across the world via satellite and reached a global audience of over 1.5 billion people in 160 countries. In a single day, the campaign received £40 million of donations for its charitable work. Among the performers were Dire Straits, Queen, Madonna, David Bowie and Mick Jagger. Live Aid demonstrated the power of music to promote awareness of problems, especially now that recent advances in technology had made it possible to reach such gigantic audiences.

Music and idealism

The lyrics of popular songs have often carried political messages, demanding change or denouncing injustice. However, such messages were less common in the music of the early 1980s, an era when the pursuit of personal wealth and happiness were emphasized. The mood was reflected in the light-hearted music of the New Romantics, including popular performers like Duran Duran and Wham! A group such as Frankie Goes to Hollywood was exceptional in

Live Aid performers take the stage together for the concert finale. Among those who can be seen are Paul McCartney, Freddie Mercury, David Bowie, Howard Jones, Adam Ant and Bob Geldof.

raising issues such as the threat of nuclear war. American hip-hop acts also took a new direction by drawing attention to the plight of inner-city black people. But the big breakthrough was the release of the 1984 Band Aid single 'Do They Know It's Christmas?', produced by Bob Geldof to raise money for starving Ethiopians. Its success was the inspiration for the Live Aid event the following year.

New media

In the 1980s, changes in technology reshaped the music industry. Acts in one country could now be seen across the globe. A new satellite channel, Music Television (MTV), transmitted music videos continuously and it became essential for singles to be supported by an eye-catching video. Also in the 1980s, music managers began to artificially create certain acts, selecting the members and moulding their look, music and style to appeal to a particular market. While the global exposure provided by videos allowed new acts to reach unprecedented audiences, the arrival of CDs (compact discs) gave older performers the opportunity to resell their albums, and the music industry boomed.

Some of the 90,000 rock fans watching the American portion of the Live Aid Concert at John F Kennedy Stadium in Philadelphia.

⊙ eye witness

There was a tremendous feeling of oneness on that stage. There had been no rivalry, no bitching, no displays of temperament all day. Now everyone was singing. They had their arms around each other.... Elton [John] was crying, everyone was crying. Not the easy tears of showbiz but genuine emotion.... The performance was still a shambles but perhaps the audience were prepared for that.... Well, the world sang it. 'Feed the World' exploded out of that stadium and literally shot around the planet.... It was a moment that let millions live. 'Remember this day,' I wrote later.

Bob Geldof, *Is That It?* (Sidgwick and Jackson, 1986)

- **SEE ALSO**
  Pages 12–13: 12 August 1981
  The IBM PC is Released

- **FURTHER INFORMATION**
  📖 Books:
  Disco, Punk, New Wave, Heavy Metal, and More: Music in the 1970s and 1980s by Michael Ray (Rosen Education Service, 2012)
  Websites:
  www.bbc.co.uk/music/thelive8event/liveaid/history.shtml
  Memories of the Live Aid concert

Space Shuttle Challenger Disintegrates

At 11.38 a.m. on 28 January 1986, the latest American space mission was launched. It ended in tragedy 73 seconds later. The space shuttle Challenger broke up at a height of 15 kilometres and a speed of about 3,500 kilometres per hour. The shuttle's crew of seven were killed. Among them was a schoolteacher, Christa McAuliffe, chosen as the first civilian to be sent into space. The Challenger crew were the first Americans to die in space. The disaster led to questions being asked about NASA's safety procedures and the future of the space shuttle programme.

A thick cloud of engine exhaust, solid rocket booster plume, and expanding gas fill the sky above the Kennedy Space Center in Florida after the explosion of the space shuttle Challenger, which claimed the lives of seven crew members.

Why it happened

The cause of the disaster turned out to be a faulty seal (O-ring) on one of the shuttle's booster rockets. A tongue of flame escaped, as video footage of the launch revealed. The breach in the booster disrupted the external fuel tank and caused the craft to break up. NASA later admitted that the booster rockets had no sensors to warn of problems. Moreover, the launch was allowed to proceed even though some engineers expressed their concern about the low temperature on launch day – the O-ring component that failed could not be relied upon if it was too cold. The mission had already been rescheduled several times as a result of delays and bad weather. The huge cost of the space programme meant that repeated delays and failures would strengthen the case of critics who saw it as a waste of resources. So on 28 January, NASA decided to ignore the doubters and proceed – with catastrophic results.

The shuttle suspended

The shuttle was introduced in 1981 as a re-useable space vehicle, differing from earlier spacecraft in its ability to leave earth and return intact. Until 1986 it had enjoyed an excellent record. Following the accident, shuttle flights were suspended while an investigation took place. Part of the blame was attributed to NASA's faulty internal communications and decision-making processes. The disaster was a blow to confidence in the space programme, and it was almost three years before another shuttle was launched.

However, there were also positive developments in the exploration of space during the 1980s, notably the journeys made by the unmanned probes Voyager I and Voyager II. Launched back in 1977, the Voyager probes sent back the first high-resolution images of Saturn (1980–1981), Uranus (1986) and Neptune (1989), planets in the outer regions of the solar system.

The seven-person crew of the Challenger included the first civilian selected to go into space, Christa McAuliffe (back row, second from the left).

What the papers said

The Challenger lifted off flawlessly this morning … for what was to have been the 25th mission…. The ship rose for about a minute on a column of smoke and fire from its five engines. Suddenly, without warning, it erupted in a ball of flame…. The eerie beauty of the orange fireball and billowing white trails … confused many onlookers…. There were few sobs, moans or shouts among the thousands of tourists, reporters, and space agency officials … just a stunned silence as they began to realize that the Challenger had vanished.

William J Broad, *New York Times*, 28 Jan 1986

- **FURTHER INFORMATION**
- Books:
  The Challenger 1986
  by Liz Gogerly (Raintree, 2007)
- Websites:
  www.nasa.gov/mission_pages/shuttle/
  shuttlemissions/archives/sts-51L.html
  Nasa's own account of the disaster

Accident at Chernobyl

The world's worst nuclear accident occurred at the Chernobyl nuclear power plant in Ukraine, in the southern Soviet Union, on 26 April 1986. A reactor at the plant exploded, and deadly radioactive material escaped. At first the Soviet authorities tried to keep the disaster secret. Four days passed before they admitted that there had been an 'incident', and even then they downplayed its seriousness. However, the rest of the world quickly became aware of it. Unusually high radiation levels were observed in Scandinavia, and US satellite photos revealed that the top of the reactor had been blown off. Soviet fire fighters struggled to contain the blaze. Lacking proper protective equipment, many of them died from the effects of the radiation. Efforts to contain the disaster and prevent it from spreading continued into mid-May.

Global fears

On 14 May the Soviet leader, Mikhail Gorbachev, appeared on television. He admitted that 299 people had been killed in the explosion and that many more were suffering from radiation exposure. Winds carried the radioactive matter across the Soviet border into northern Europe. Scandinavia and Finland were particularly badly affected, and the Sami people of the far north found their entire way of life threatened when the

Disaster at Chernobyl: at the nuclear power plant in Ukraine, the overheating core of reactor number 4 caused the entire roof to be blown off the building.

These apples, hanging from a tree near Chernobyl, were visibly contaminated as a result of the disaster at the city's nuclear plant. The city itself had to be abandoned and is still a ghost town.

⊙ eye witness

We were newlyweds.... We lived in the fire station where he worked.... One night I heard a noise. I looked out the window. He saw me.... 'Go back to sleep. There's a fire at the reactor. I'll be back soon.' I didn't see the explosion itself. Just the flames. Everything was radiant. The whole sky. A tall flame. And smoke. The heat was awful.... At seven in the morning I was told he was in the hospital. He was all swollen and puffed up.... I tell the nurse: 'He's dying.' And she says: 'What did you expect? He got 1,600 roentgen. Four hundred is a lethal dose.'

Lyudmilla Ignatenko, in Svetlana Alexievich, _Voices from Chernobyl_ (Dalkey Archive, 2005)

reindeer on which they depended became contaminated. European governments placed restrictions on the movement and sale of livestock and other products. Some of these restrictions were still in force 20 years later.

Dangerous power

Chernobyl was not the first nuclear accident. Many smaller incidents had occurred in the past. In 1979 there was a major alarm at Three Mile Island in Pennsylvania, USA, which caused the United States to suspend its programme of building new power stations. Chernobyl was truly disastrous, however. The entire area around the power station, including the city of Chernobyl, had to be evacuated and sealed off.

The long-term effects of the accident were much disputed. One report gave a low figure of 4,000 deaths worldwide resulting from the accident. Others suggested that radiation, responsible for cancers and birth defects, had had a huge impact across Europe.

In 2011 the second-worst nuclear accident occurred in Fukishima, Japan, when three reactors exploded after being damaged by a tsunami. The accident led to renewed concern about the safety of nuclear power.

- **SEE ALSO**
Pages 22–23: 11 March 1985
Gorbachev Becomes Soviet Leader

- **FURTHER INFORMATION**
  📖 Books:
  Chernobyl Disaster
  by Marcia Amidon Lusted
  (Essential Library, 2011)
  Websites:
  library.thinkquest.org/3426/
  A comprehensive site about the disaster

World Stock Exchanges Crash

19 October 1987 is remembered as 'Black Monday', a day that witnessed a huge drop in the value of shares in financial markets across the world. The fall began on Friday 16 October with heavy selling on Wall Street in New York City, the principal US stock exchange and the world's most influential centre of finance. When large numbers of people want to get rid of their shares, prices fall and the shares are worth less. If the selling continues, share values fall low enough to hurt or even ruin individuals and companies. This was what happened after stock exchanges re-opened on Monday morning. The selling continued and share prices fell in Tokyo, London, Hong Kong and Wall Street.

Shock and fear

The crash was so severe that people feared there would be a world depression. This had happened in 1929, when the Wall Street Crash triggered a shrinking of the world economy and mass unemployment. Fortunately, in 1987 the follow-up to Black Monday proved to be less disastrous. Afterwards, there was no agreement as to the cause of the crash. Over-rapid expansion and an over-optimism that pushed prices too high were common explanations. Some blamed recently installed computer systems that were pre-programmed to buy and sell shares.

Frantic traders on the floor of the Sydney Stock Exchange try to sell off their shares before the close of trading. More than 60 billion Australian dollars were wiped off the market's value in one day, a record in the history of the exchange.

What the papers said

The rumors mounted by the hour as Wall Street lunged and lurched through its wildest week. Many of the country's biggest … firms … were said to be in trouble, even sinking…. Even before Black Monday struck, there were signs that Wall Street's five-year stay in Fat City was ending. Profits were shrinking…. Retrenchment [economizing] of some kind was already in the cards. Last week's crash guaranteed that it will be harsher than was previously expected. There is plenty of shrinking to do…. What had happened was, in a word, overexpansion.

John Greenwald, *Time*, 2 November 1987

They argued that this 'program trading' could lead to unwise mass selling, with disastrous results. However, there was no evidence that human traders would have behaved differently, since chain-reaction selling had often occurred in earlier crises.

Enterprise culture

During the 1980s, acquiring personal wealth became a central value for many people in Western society. President Ronald Reagan in the USA and Britain's Margaret Thatcher were particularly active in encouraging an 'enterprise culture'. They stressed the importance of risk-taking and profit-making as engines of economic growth. Critics of these values argued that they promoted selfishness and greed at the expense of social responsibility. Many people certainly did very well in this period, including the high-earning young people often described as yuppies (Young, Upwardly Mobile Professionals). Loathed by some and admired by others, the typical yuppie would wear a pinstripe suit, have slicked-back hair and drive an expensive sports car. Black Monday was a major blow to the self-assurance of these products of the enterprise culture.

Charlie Sheen in the 1987 film Wall Street. *The movie is regarded as a classic portrayal of 1980s greed. Sheen plays an ambitious yuppie.*

- **SEE ALSO**
  Pages 10–11: 4 December 1980
  Reagan is Elected US President
  Pages 12–13: 12 August 1981
  The IBM PC is Released

- **FURTHER INFORMATION**
  📖 Books:
  How the Stock Market Works
  by Kathy Furgang
  (Rosen Publishing Group, 2010)
  Websites:
  www.ft.com/indepth/blackmonday
  A site with links to videos explaining the crash

Soviet Troops Leave Afghanistan

The last remaining Soviet units in Afghanistan began to leave on 15 February 1989. Their withdrawal ended a nine-year involvement in Afghanistan's internal struggles. It began in 1979, when Afghanistan was ruled by the communist PDPA (People's Democratic Party of Afghanistan). The government was facing a widespread rebellion and needed help from its Soviet ally. But when Soviet troops arrived in force, they overthrew the Afghan government in favour of a different faction of the PDPA.

The rapid build-up of Soviet military strength in Afghanistan was internationally condemned as an invasion, but the Soviet Union appeared determined to impose communism on an unwilling people. Their actions were not unprecedented. Both Cold War rivals, the United States and the Soviet Union, had often intervened, openly or secretly, in other countries to help allied governments or topple unfriendly regimes.

Soldiers of the Soviet Union's Red Army wave to onlookers as their convoy of armoured vehicles makes its way out of Afghanistan.

⊙ eye witness

I was held at the airport for three days, in a small locked room.… I saw the last Soviet plane leave, with no ceremony and the last few gaudily made-up wives grumbling their way out across the tarmac.… I suppose it was a world exclusive as I was the only journalist there … but I had no chance of filing a story: the military might have satellite phones in the 1980s, but journalists didn't.… I had no idea if anyone knew that the last Soviet plane had left Kabul. I was in the back of the beyond.

Jeremy Bowen, *War Stories* (Simon & Schuster, 2006)

The resistance

The new, Soviet-backed government failed to win over the people. Afghanistan was an economically backward country. Its people were Muslim and fiercely independent. Most were opposed to communism and hated foreign troops. The government often acted in a clumsy and brutal fashion. Measures such as land reform and the education of women found no support outside the towns.

The Soviet and Afghan armies easily won battles against local warlords, but rebel guerrillas were a different matter. These mujahideen, or 'warriors', fought in small groups, taking advantage of Afghanistan's mountainous terrain to hit their enemies and then disappear. The United States supplied the mujahideen with anti-aircraft missiles and other weapons. Muslim fighters from other lands joined them in the fight. Like the United States in Vietnam, the Soviet Union became bogged down in a punishing and exhausting war it could not win. Eventually, the Soviet leader Mikhail Gorbachev decided to end the war. Soviet troops began to withdraw in stages from May 1988.

Mujahideen guerrillas at a machine gun nest fire at Soviet aircraft flying through the Jagdalak Valley in eastern Afghanistan.

Exit strategy

The Soviet exit was part of Gorbachev's overall strategy, intended to reduce the Soviet Union's crippling military commitments and improve relations with the West. Evacuating the Red Army was difficult, since it entailed transporting 80,000 men and large numbers of tanks and armoured vehicles over dangerous terrain. Although the Soviet Union undertook some successful missions as face-saving exercises before withdrawing, these had no influence on the conflict. The mujahideen increasingly took the offensive. The communist regime managed to fight on without Soviet help until it was overthrown in 1992.

- **SEE ALSO**
  Pages 22–23: 11 March 1985
  Gorbachev Becomes Soviet Leader

- **FURTHER INFORMATION**
  Books:
  Afghanistan by Richard Spilsbury (Wayland, 2013)
  Websites:
  www.bbc.co.uk/news/world-south-asia-12011352
  Concise profile of the recent history of Afghanistan

The Louvre 'Pyramid' Opens

The Louvre in Paris is one of France's most famous buildings. Originally a royal palace, it houses a huge national art collection, including many great paintings such as Leonardo da Vinci's 'Mona Lisa'. In 1981 the French president, François Mitterand, commissioned American architect I M Pei to design a new structure to stand in the vast courtyard of the Louvre. Pei's creation, Le Pyramide, was officially opened on 29 March 1989.

The Pyramid actually consists of one large and two much smaller pyramids, made of sparkling, reflective glass covering a grid-like steel frame. The main structure stands 21 metres high and measures 33 metres along the base of each side. It serves a practical purpose, providing a spacious entrance to the Louvre, leading down to a large, light-filled lobby. Initially many people criticized the Pyramid, feeling that its shape, materials and transparency jarred with the stately, classical style of the Louvre. However, over time, Pei's Pyramid has become a famous and familiar part of the cityscape.

The Louvre Pyramid stands as a striking symbol of modernity in the courtyard of the Louvre museum.

Parisian projects

The Pyramid was one of many new buildings erected during Mitterand's presidency (1981–1995) as part of a single, ambitious programme, Les Grands Projets (The Great Projects). They ranged from a monumental Great Arch containing offices to a modernistic park scattered with bright red buildings. A disused railway station was imaginatively transformed into a major art museum, the Musée d'Orsay (1986). And the Arab World Institute (1987), designed by Jean Nouvel, had an extraordinary south front filled with aluminium and glass panels. Thousands of 'diaphragms' opened and closed in them, appearing and disappearing. They controlled the amount of light allowed into the building while also creating a fascinating visual spectacle.

1980s buildings

By the 1980s, there was no single dominant style in architecture. New buildings often mixed styles, and advances in engineering enabled architects to produce highly unusual designs. The AT&T Building in New York (1984), designed by veteran American architect Philip Johnson, was a conventional skyscraper built in pink granite and decorated with pseudo-classical features. By contrast, the British architect Richard Rogers gave the Lloyds Building (1986), in the City of London, fantasy-like tall metal towers constructed around a central space, with pipes, lifts and other utility features exposed on the outside. Such glamorous commercial projects were undertaken in many of the world's major cities and fitted the dynamic atmosphere of the 1980s.

La Grande Arche in west Paris was designed by Danish architect Johann Otto von Spreckelsen.

What the papers said

Ieoh Ming Pei ... designed a ... pyramid which, surmounting a grand underground entrance hall, has become a bigger spectacle than the Mona Lisa, and Paris's most controversial piece of modern architecture.... Though early reactions to the pyramid ranged from the amazed to the hostile, Mr Pei remained confident that Parisians would learn to love his structure ... when they could see how useful a role it played in creating big, bright spaces below, and how reordering the museum around a new point of entry gave its rambling galleries a more logical and accessible shape.

Robert Cottrell, *Independent*, March 30, 1989.

• **FURTHER INFORMATION**

📖 **Books:**
I.M. Pei: Architect of Time, Place and Purpose
by Jil Rubalcaba
(Amazon Children's Publishing, 2011)

🖱 **Websites:**
www.louvre.fr/en/rooms/cour-napoleon-0
Louvre site with virtual tour of Pyramid

04
JUNE
1989

Massacre in Tiananmen Square

Demonstrations in China's capital, Beijing, ended on 4 June 1989 when army units moved in and fired on the protesters, many of them students. The demonstrations were focused in and around the historic centre, Tiananmen Square. The protests, attended by up to 100,000 people, had faced China's ruling Communist Party with a difficult decision. The leadership was split, since elements within the party and the army had some sympathy with the demonstrators. But the hardliners took control and used troops to crack down on dissent.

A new atmosphere

China had been ruled by the Communist Party since 1949. The communists, led by Mao Zedong, had established a powerful one-party state. Mao's 27-year rule was marked by often disastrous experiments that damaged China's society, economy and foreign relations. His successor, Deng Xiaoping, set the country on a different course. People were encouraged to go into business for themselves, and foreign firms began to operate in China. The new atmosphere encouraged people's hopes for greater political freedom. They were further encouraged by Mikhail Gorbachev's reforms in the Soviet Union. Gorbachev's visit to China in April 1989 sparked the demonstrations in Tiananmen Square.

During the demonstrations, students carved a statue of the 'Goddess of Democracy', a woman holding aloft a torch, which strongly resembled the famous Statue of Liberty in New York Harbor. Despite the hint of US influence, the protesters may not have wanted to see China transformed

The assembled demonstrators hail the statue of the 'Goddess of Democracy' in Tiananmen Square.

into a Western-style democracy. Nevertheless, they certainly hoped for greater openness and opportunities to express their opinions.

Just an incident?

The details of what actually occurred on 4 June are still unclear. The West immediately described it as 'the Tiananmen Square massacre'. To the Chinese authorities it was 'the June 4 Incident'. Estimates of the number of dead vary wildly. The Chinese claimed that no student protesters were killed, only troublemakers who had tried to take advantage of the disorder. However, Western foreign correspondents in Beijing claimed that at least 2,000 civilians were killed. Whatever the truth is, the Chinese government's actions that day demonstrated that, unlike East European communist governments in 1989, it had no intention of giving way to popular protest. Despite tremendous economic growth and ever-increasing contacts with the outside world, China would continue into the 21st century as a tightly controlled single-party state.

A lone protester, known to the world as 'Tank Man', heroically blocks the path of a tank convoy along the Avenue of Eternal Peace near Tiananmen Square.

◉ eye witness

At four o'clock sharp, just before daybreak, the lights in the Square suddenly went out ... the front of the Square was packed with troops ... they lined up ... machine-guns in front of the Monument to the Heroes of the People.... The troops and policemen ... stormed the monument.... Some troops were kneeling down and firing. We had to retreat back up onto the Monument. When we reached it the machine-guns stopped. But the troops on the Monument beat us back down again. As soon as we'd been beaten down, the machine-guns started up again ... we escaped in the direction of Beijing railway station.

An anonymous Beijing student, New Statesman and Society, 16 June 1989

- **SEE ALSO**
  Pages 16–17: 16 September 1982
  Massacres in Lebanon
  Pages 38–39: 10 November 1989
  The Berlin Wall Comes Down

- **FURTHER INFORMATION**
  📖 Books:
  Days that Shook the World: Tiananmen Square by Jane Bingham (Hodder Children's Books, 2012)
  🖰 Websites:
  http://news.bbc.co.uk/onthisday/hi/dates/stories/june/4/newsid_2496000/2496277.stm
  Story from the BBC on the day of the massacre

The Berlin Wall Comes Down

On 10 November, for the first time in 28 years, East Germans crossed freely into West Berlin. Since 1961, West Berlin had been fenced off by a 3.5-metre-high concrete wall policed by armed guards ready to shoot anyone who tried to climb over it. The object of the wall was to prevent citizens of communist East Germany from fleeing to West Berlin, a small non-communist area deep inside East German territory. However, by 1989, the political situation was changing. On 9 November the East German authorities announced that the previously guarded checkpoints would be opened. Huge numbers of jubilant East Germans crossed the border. Many of them demolished sections of the hated wall and took away chunks as souvenirs. The event came to be called the fall of the Berlin Wall. Though it did not literally disappear, it had ceased to keep people apart.

East Germans eagerly clamber over the Berlin Wall after learning that they could cross freely into West Berlin for the first time.

Europe divided

Germany was divided in 1945, as each of the major victorious Allies of World War II took control of one zone. Eventually the US, British and French zones were united as West Germany (the Federal Republic). The Soviet-held eastern zone became a communist state, East Germany (the German Democratic Republic). The pre-war German capital, Berlin, deep in the eastern zone, was similarly divided into West Berlin (part of the Federal Republic) and East Berlin.

● eye witness

There was activity all along the Wall, and the constant sound of hammering. People were beating the Wall with picks and chisels. The candles they brought shed a golden light.... When the men ... stopped hitting the Wall on our side, you could still hear sounds ... people were trying to break through from the Eastern side ... a tiny hole appeared, and then grew bigger. At last, we saw a hand come through the little gap.... A man on our side grabbed it and shook it. In all my life I had never thought anything like this might ... be possible.

John Simpson, *Twenty Tales from the War Zone* (Pan, 2007)

November 1989: Huge crowds of demonstrators gather in Prague, capital of the former Czechoslovakia, to demand change and to protest against the unpopular communist regime.

By this time, the Cold War had begun and a long frontier, nicknamed the 'Iron Curtain', separated Western and Eastern Europe. Though stranded behind the Iron Curtain, West Berlin survived, and its existence caused the communist regime serious problems.

The curtain lifts

As in other Eastern European states, East Germany's communist government had been imposed by the Soviet army at the end of World War II. It was never popular, and huge numbers of East Germans fled by crossing into West Berlin. Finally, in 1961, the Berlin Wall was built to prevent further mass migrations. The wall served its purpose until Mikhail Gorbachev withdrew Soviet protection from East Germany and the other communist regimes in the late 1980s. In 1989 mass popular protests led to changes of government in Poland and Hungary. As the pressure built up, East Germany accepted the inevitable, and the wall came down. The tide of revolution swept on. By the end of 1989 East European communism had collapsed.

- **SEE ALSO**
Pages 6–7: 30 August 1980
Solidarity is Legalized in Poland
Pages 22–23: 11 March 1985
Gorbachev Becomes Soviet Leader
Pages 36–37: 4 June 1989
Massacre in Tiananmen Square

- **FURTHER INFORMATION**
Books:
The Fall of the Berlin Wall
edited by Jeff T Hay (Greenhaven Press, 2009)
Websites:
www.germany.info/relaunch/info/publications/
infocus/9_November/wall_stories37.html
Personal recollections of the fall of the Berlin Wall

The SAS Storm the Iranian Embassy

On 30 April 1980, terrorists took over the Iranian embassy in London. Five days later, the Special Air Service (SAS), a special forces unit of the British army, launched an assault on the embassy. They freed 19 of the 20 hostages taken captive by the terrorists. Five of the terrorists and one hostage were killed during the operation, codenamed Nimrod. Previously little known, the SAS were hailed as heroes.

The terrorists' aims

The crisis began when the six-man terrorist team captured the embassy in South Kensington, central London. They belonged to a group called the Democratic Revolutionary Movement for the Liberation of Arabistan. Arabistan was the group's name for the province of Khuzestan in southern Iran. Unlike most of Iran, Khuzestan has a large Arab population, and the group wished to break away from Iran. They had strong ties with neighbouring Iraq, an Arab country. In fact, it was later revealed that Iraq had armed and trained the terrorists. Iraq's leader, Saddam Hussein, was planning a war with Iran. One of his objectives was to take over Khuzestan.

Stalemate

The terrorists demanded the release of members of their movement in Iranian prisons. They threatened to kill their hostages if their demands weren't met. For a week, as the world's media watched and waited, there was stalemate. Then, on 5 May, the terrorists became impatient and executed a hostage, Iranian Press Secretary Abbas Lavansani. The victim's body was thrown down the steps outside

⊙ eye witness

On that Monday, things hotted up; shots were heard, and a body was pushed out of the front door.... We had no inkling of the horrible scene in the embassy, with tensions boiling over, guns held to hostages' heads and the smell of fear everywhere ... the first stun grenade explosion occurred.... As black smoke billowed from a first-floor window, the police ... ran back and forth telling people to lie on the ground ... a microphone appeared snaking towards me.... I stuck to telling what I could see, though my imagination was racing. This was the SAS.

Kate Adie, *The Kindness of Strangers* (Headline, 2002)

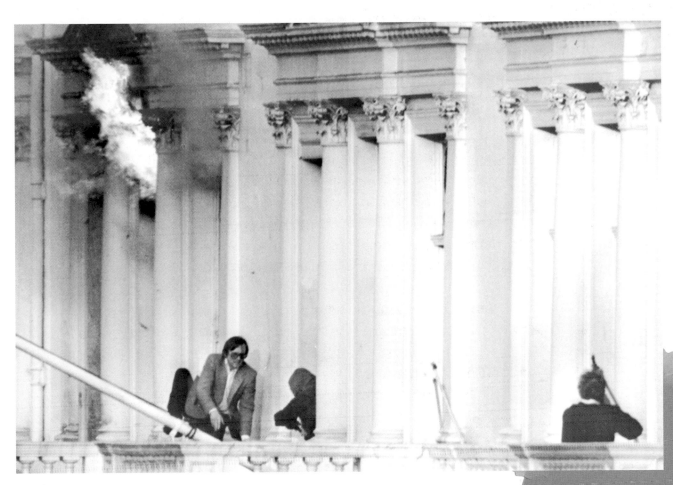

the building. The gunmen threatened to slay one hostage every 30 minutes. At this point the British government decided that they had to use force to end the siege.

Operation Nimrod

The SAS, a regiment of the British army with specialized combat skills, was sent in. The soldiers wore black uniforms and balaclavas and were armed with sub-machine guns. They attacked from two sides. Some blew open the front first-floor windows with explosives while others abseiled from the roof to enter the rear of the building. They tossed stun grenades inside to disorient the terrorists, then moved swiftly through the rooms, killing the terrorists one by one. In the confusion a second hostage, an Iranian diplomat, died. One of the hostages, Trevor Lock, a British policeman, assisted the SAS. His courage earned him the George Medal. The rescue operation was praised as a great feat of arms and a heartening victory over terrorism.

Sim Harris (left), a BBC sound recordist taken hostage while visiting the embassy, escapes across a balcony, guarded by an SAS commando, during Operation Nimrod.

- **SEE ALSO**
  Pages 8–9: 22 September 1980
  Iran and Iraq Go to War

- **FURTHER INFORMATION**
  📖 Books:
  Special Forces by Adam Sutherland
  (Wayland, 2012)
  🖱 Websites:
  www.eliteukforces.info/special-air-service/
  sas-operations/iranian-embassy/
  A site about the siege with some dramatic photos

12 MARCH 1984

The Coal Miners' Strike Begins

In March 1984, the chairman of the National Coal Board, Ian MacGregor, announced that 20 unprofitable pits would be closed down. The move would cost 20,000 miners' jobs, many of them in areas such as Yorkshire and South Wales, where entire communities lived from the mining industry. Opposing the decision, Arthur Scargill, the president of the National Union of Mineworkers (NUM), called a national strike, to begin on 12 March. The strike lasted almost a year before the miners admitted defeat. It caused intense bitterness and marked the beginning of a major decline in the mining industry.

The opponents

Coal had been a major industry for 200 years, vital to Britain's economic development. The miners were traditionally a militant workforce, and had been involved in many trade disputes. In the early 1970s, national coal strikes had achieved their aims and had been partly responsible for the fall of Edward Heath's Conservative government in 1974. However, in 1984 the miners faced a more formidable Conservative leader, Margaret Thatcher. She was determined to reduce the power of British trade unions and had already passed laws to limit their activities. Taking on the NUM would be a crucial test of her government's strength.

Arthur Scargill, the president of the National Union of Mineworkers, addresses his striking supporters.

The long struggle

The NUM's position had serious weaknesses. The strike was called at the end of winter when coal was less in demand. Moreover, the government had stockpiled coal reserves in readiness. The miners themselves were disunited. Scargill put himself at a disadvantage by refusing to hold a ballot (vote) on strike action. The majority were willing to strike, but some whose jobs were not threatened preferred to work on. They were particularly strong in Nottinghamshire, where miners broke away from the NUM and formed a separate union. Yorkshire miners travelled to Nottinghamshire in an effort to prevent work from continuing, breaking new laws which prohibited such 'secondary picketing'.

As the strike went on, attitudes hardened, and there were some violent clashes between striking miners and police. Even when Scargill finally accepted defeat and ended the strike on 3 March 1985, some miners felt betrayed and wanted to go on. Subsequently, Scargill's claims that many more closures were planned were shown to be correct. Britain's coal mining industry rapidly wound down. Mrs Thatcher's victory strengthened her prestige and greatly weakened the trade union movement in Britain.

British police surround protesting coalminers. There were some violent clashes between miners and police during the strike.

What the papers said

If there is bitterness [among miners] against Ian MacGregor, there is also bitterness against Arthur Scargill for trying to bring men out without a national strike ballot. Either way, now, the mood in the mines is both menacing and unpredictable. With spring almost here and coal stocks high, action intended to batter Mr MacGregor into submission could degenerate into a civil war of miner versus miner. Under its present leadership, the union that brought down governments is this time in real danger of smashing itself to smithereens.

Daily Mail, 12 March 1984

- **SEE ALSO**
  Pages 6–7: 30 August 1980
  Solidarity is Legalized in Poland

- **FURTHER INFORMATION**
  Books:
  Coal: Opposing Viewpoints
  edited by Roman Espejo
  (Greenhaven Press, 2011)
  Websites:
  www.num.org.uk/?p=history&c=num&h=13
  History of the strike from the miners' perspective

The Lockerbie Disaster

On 21 December 1988, Pan Am Flight 103 was on its way from Frankfurt to New York's JFK airport. At 7.02 p.m., less than an hour after a scheduled stop at London Heathrow, the plane crashed on the small Scottish town of Lockerbie. All 259 people on board were killed, together with 11 people on the ground. It was the worst air disaster in British history. Witnesses described the craft falling out of the sky in a rain of fire. The wreckage was strewn across the town and the surrounding area. Buildings and cars caught fire, and in one street, Sherwood Crescent, houses were destroyed by the impact of the detached wings. Helicopters flew in medical teams while firefighters battled the flames.

The battered cockpit of Pan Am Flight 103 lies in a field near Lockerbie following the terrorist attack that killed all 259 passengers. The bombing led airlines to tighten their security.

The explosion

At first, no one knew what had caused the plane to break apart, but a terrorist bomb was immediately suspected. Crash retrieval experts arrived to examine the remaining evidence. The flight recorders, known as 'black boxes', failed to shed any light on events, but experts eventually confirmed that the plane had indeed been brought down by a bomb. A plastic explosive device had been smuggled into the cargo hold. The detonation had ripped a hole in the plane, which caused it to disintegrate. Evidence from the wreckage showed that no emergency procedures had been carried out on the plane, indicating that it had been destroyed almost instantly.

Responsibility

The majority of the passengers were Americans, including soldiers and CIA (Central Intelligence Agency) employees. This suggested that the bomb may have been been planted by anti-American terrorists. The British police and the American FBI worked closely together and identified two employees of Libyan Arab Airlines as the probable culprits. The investigators suspected that Libya may have staged the attacks in retaliation for earlier US attacks on Libyan boats and aircraft. Eventually, in 1999, Libya allowed the suspects to be sent to Britain. At their trial, only one of the men was found guilty. Over the following years, he continued to claim that he was innocent. The Libyan government never admitted its involvement in the attack, although it accepted responsibility for its officials' deeds and paid compensation to the victims' families. Rightly or wrongly, many people remained convinced that the full story had yet to be revealed.

Falling pieces of the plane destroyed houses on the ground, as shown in this photograph.

⊙ eye witness

I had been upstairs getting ready to go out to bingo ... when I heard the sound of a low-flying jet.... I actually thought it was going to hit the house, and started running down the stairs. As I reached the hall, my husband grabbed me and pushed me up against the wall. He said, 'It's an earthquake.' I opened the front door and we went outside. As we reached the doorstep, there was a huge explosion across the town. I could feel the heat on my face. It was searing, like putting your face in front of a blazing fire.

Margaret Cameron, in David Johnston, Lockerbie: The Real Story (Bloomsbury, 1989)

- **SEE ALSO**
  Pages 26–27: 28 January 1986
  Space Shuttle Challenger Disintegrates

  Pages 40–41: 5 May 1980
  The SAS Storm the Iranian Embassy

- **FURTHER INFORMATION**
  📖 Books:
  Terrorist File: The Lockerbie Investigation by Amanda Howard (Bearport Publishing, 2007)
  🖱 Websites:
  www.cbc.ca/news/background/lockerbie/index.html
  Site covering the disaster, investigation and trials

People of the Decade

Yasser Arafat
(1929–2004)
A Palestinian leader who, in 1969, became chairman of the Palestine Liberation Organization (PLO), bringing together most of the militant Palestinian groups hostile to Israel. Despite PLO terrorism, Arafat addressed the United Nations and skilfully publicized the Palestinian cause. After years of changing fortunes, in 1993 Arafat made a peace agreement with Israeli leaders that allowed for limited Palestinian self-rule in the occupied territories. In 1994 he became president of the Palestinian National Authority, but violent new conflicts troubled his later years.

Benazir Bhutto
(1953–2007)
The first woman to lead a modern Muslim state, Benazir Bhutto became prime minister of Pakistan in 1988–1990 and 1993–1996. As head of the Pakistan People's Party, she was opposed by conservative elements in Pakistan and by the army, which often intervened in politics. Both of her terms in office were controversially cut short. In exile from 1996, she returned to Pakistan in October 2007 but was assassinated two months later.

Deng Xiaoping
(1904–1997)
A veteran communist, Deng Xiaoping held high government office in China from the 1950s. Favouring moderate, realistic policies, Deng was in disgrace during the Cultural Revolution, launched in 1966 by China's leader, Mao Zedong. Deng gradually rebuilt his position, and after Mao's death (1976) he became Chinese leader and introduced new policies allowing more economic freedom. China prospered, but power remained with the Communist Party, which crushed the 1989 protest movement in Tiananmen Square.

Diana, Princess of Wales
(1961–1997)
In 1981 Lady Diana Spencer married the heir to the British throne, Charles, Prince of Wales, in a televised ceremony watched by a global audience of 750 million. The royal marriage quickly ran into difficulties, and Charles and Diana were finally divorced in 1996. However, Diana remained a popular figure, often in the news and admired for her charitable work. Her death in a car accident in 1997 sparked an astonishing display of public mourning.

Madonna
(1958–)
A musician and actress, Madonna became a pop sensation in the 1980s. She released her debut album in 1983 and went on to produce three number-one albums before 1990. She had a strong influence on young people's outlook and fashions, and the lyrics of songs such as 'Material Girl' reflected the decade's emphasis on affluence and possessions. Often referred to as the 'Queen of Pop', Madonna maintained her superstar status into the 21st century.

Ferdinand Marcos
(1917–1989)
In 1965 Marcos was elected president of the Philippines in South-East Asia. Increasingly corrupt and dictatorial, he enriched himself while millions of Filipinos lived in poverty; the huge, gaudy shoe collection of his wife Imelda became particularly notorious. In 1986 Marcos was forced to hold an election following the assassination of a political rival, Benigno Aquino. Marcos claimed to have won, but popular anger forced him into exile, and the murdered man's widow, Corazon Aquino, became president.

François Mitterrand
(1916–1996)
Mitterand was president of France for a record 14 years (1981–1995), winning elections in 1981 and 1988 as the candidate of the Socialist Party. He strongly supported closer ties with Germany and other European powers and was a key player in the formation of the European Union in 1993. He also launched an ambitious building programme that transformed large areas of the capital, Paris.

Martina Navratilova
(1956–)
The tennis star Navratilova left her home country of Czechoslovakia in 1975 and settled in the USA. She won the singles at Wimbledon in 1978 and dominated women's tennis for over a decade. During her career, she captured 167 championship titles, more than any other player, male or female, in history. She retired in 1994, making a brief return to doubles competitions in 2000. At a time when public figures revealed little about their sexuality, she became an outspoken campaigner for gay rights.

Oprah Winfrey
(1954–)
Coming from a poor background, Winfrey became one of the world's most influential women and the richest African American. Her talk show, *The Oprah Winfrey Show* ran from 1984 to 2011. It maintained a huge audience and Winfrey took up important issues, such as drug abuse, and raised money for many causes, including help for New Orleans following Hurricane Katrina. She launched her own media channel, the Oprah Winfrey Network, in 2011.

Glossary

abseiling Descending the sheer face of a rock or building, using double ropes.

autonomy Self-government that falls short of independence. Scotland and Wales, for example, run many of their own affairs but are finally answerable to the British parliament in Westminster (London).

bloc A group of states that are allies and generally act together.

CIA The Central Intelligence Agency, the organization that undertakes information gathering and espionage for the US government.

Cold War The long period of hostility (roughly 1945–1990) between the United States and the Soviet Union, and their respective allies. It is described as 'cold' because there was no actual fighting between the two main powers, but a tense battle for influence and military superiority.

colony A territory ruled by a distant and usually more powerful state. India and Nigeria were British colonies, and so were the 13 American colonies that revolted and formed the United States.

communism A political and economic system in which wealth and production are controlled by the state, supposedly for the benefit of all citizens.

conscript A citizen who must undertake compulsory military service.

decrepit Worn out through age.

depression A long-lasting economic crisis involving declining production, bank failures and mass unemployment.

dictatorship A form of government in which a single person or small group has absolute power.

epidemic An outbreak of a disease that spreads quickly and more widely than would normally be expected. The World Health Organization declared Aids an epidemic in the 1980s.

FBI The Federal Bureau of Investigation is a bureau of the US Department of Justice that deals with matters of national security, federal crimes and crimes against the government.

guerrillas Fighters who avoid open warfare, instead launching surprise attacks and then withdrawing quickly. Guerrilla tactics are particularly effective in difficult terrain such as mountains or jungles.

livestock Domestic animals that are kept for food or similar purposes.

martial law Military law, often imposed on an entire population during a real or pretended emergency.

militancy This describes the vigorous, sometimes violent, pursuit of political or other aims.

militia Citizens who are organized to fight but are not full-time soldiers.

mujahideen A term for Muslim fighters engaged in holy war (jihad), especially those who opposed the Soviet-backed regime in Afghanistan between 1980 and 1988.

NASA The National Aeronautics and Space Administration, the organization responsible for the US space programme.

PLO The Palestinian Liberation Organization. It consists of a number of groups formerly dedicated to destroying Israel and now aiming to establish a Palestinian state.

radioactive This describes material that sends out radiation. Radiation is energy in the form of sub-atomic particles that are harmful to living things.

Red Army The army of the Soviet Union.

Republican A member or supporter of the Republican Party, one of the USA's two main political parties. The other is the Democratic Party.

Roentgen A measure of radiation (see radioactive).

Royal Marines A unit of Britain's Royal Navy with specialist commando training.

sanctions Limits on trade with a particular country, usually imposed by the international community on regimes that behave unacceptably.

SAS The Special Air Service, a special forces unit of the British Army. Its responsibilities include counter-terrorist operations.

shares Any of the equal parts into which ownership of a company is divided.

skirmish A small-scale fight, involving fewer men than a battle. Skirmishes often happen as a result of accidental clashes in which no clear military objective is involved.

Soviet Union Also called the USSR (Union of Soviet Socialist Republics), the Soviet Union was founded in 1922 as a communist state encompassing Russia and other nearby countries. It collapsed in 1991.

stagnant Not moving. The word is used in economics to describe lack of progress.

stalemate A situation in which neither of two opposing sides can gain the advantage.

strike A form of action undertaken by employees who refuse to work until their pay or working conditions are improved.

trade union An organization that represents some or all of the workers in a particular industry.

unilateral One-sided; a decision reached without the agreement of another concerned party.

Index

Page numbers in **bold** refer to illustrations